First Facts™

Health Matters

Head Lice

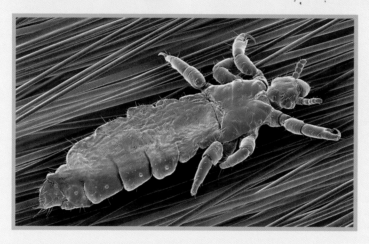

by Jason Glaser

Consultant:
James R. Hubbard, MD
Fellow in the American Academy of Pediatrics
Iowa Medical Society
West Des Moines, Iowa

Capstone press
Mankato, Minnesota

First Facts is published by Capstone Press,
151 Good Counsel Drive, P.O. Box 669, Mankato, Minnesota 56002.
www.capstonepress.com

Library of Congress Cataloging-in-Publication Data
Glaser, Jason.
  Head lice / by Jason Glaser.
    p. cm.—(First facts. Health matters)
    Summary: "Introduces head lice, its causes, symptoms, and treatments"—Provided
by publisher.
    Includes bibliographical references and index.
    ISBN 0-7368-4291-8 (hardcover)
    1. Pediculosis—Juvenile literature. I. Title. II. Series.
RL764.P4G56 2006
616.5'72—dc22   2004031053

Editorial Credits
Mari C. Schuh, editor; Juliette Peters, designer; Kelly Garvin, photo researcher/photo editor

Photo Credits
Capstone Press/Karon Dubke, cover (foreground), 10, 11, 14, 15, 19, 20, 21
Corbis/Rolf Bruderer, 8
Getty Images Inc./Mike Powell, 9
Photo Researchers Inc./Eye of Science, 5; Mark Clarke, 6–7; Science Photo Library/
    St. Bartholomew's Hospital, 16
Visuals Unlimited/Deb Yeske, 12–13; Dr. Dennis Kunkel, 1, cover (background)

1 2 3 4 5 6 10 09 08 07 06 05

Table of Contents

What Are Head Lice?

Head lice are tiny bugs that live in hair. Head lice suck blood from people's skin. Female lice lay eggs called **nits** in hair. The nits hatch to become head lice. Head lice can live up to a month on a person's head.

Fact!
Female lice can lay up to 100 eggs each.

4

head louse seen through a microscope

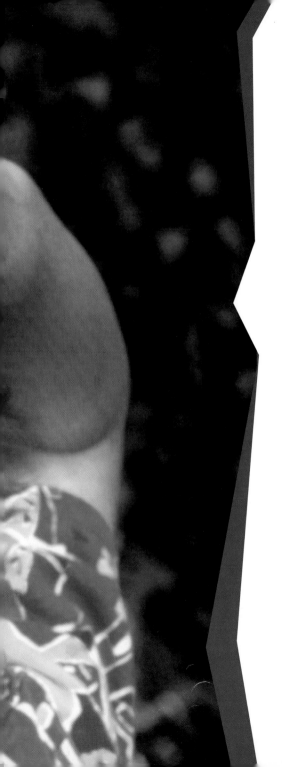

Signs of Head Lice

Lice bite the skin on people's heads. The bites leave red spots and can sometimes itch.

Nits look like white flecks. They stick to hair. People can see nits and lice on someone's head.

Fact!

Head lice cannot fly or jump. They have to crawl onto a person's head from somewhere else.

How Do Kids Get Lice?

Kids get head lice from other people. Head lice sometimes spread during hugs or other contact.

Head lice can crawl onto anything a
person's head touches. They get onto
pillowcases, combs, hats, or clothes.
Sharing these things can pass head lice.

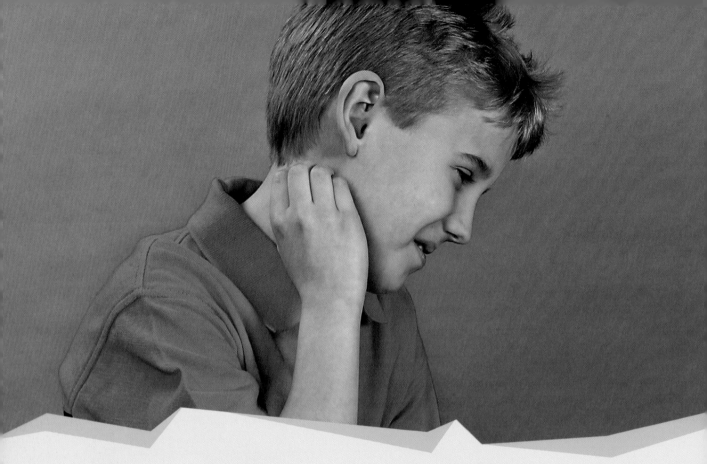

What Else Could It Be?

An itchy head is not always head lice. Mosquito bites, dry skin, and **allergies** can cause itchy heads. Fleas can also hide in hair. Flea bites itch too.

Drops of hair spray and white specks called **dandruff** can look like nits. Hair spray and dandruff can be shaken out. Nits must be picked out of hair.

Should Kids See a Doctor?

Kids do not need to see a doctor for head lice. Going to the doctor may spread lice to others. Head lice can be treated at home. Kids should stay home from school until their head lice are gone.

Fact!
Anyone can get head lice. It is not true that people who don't wash are more likely to get head lice.

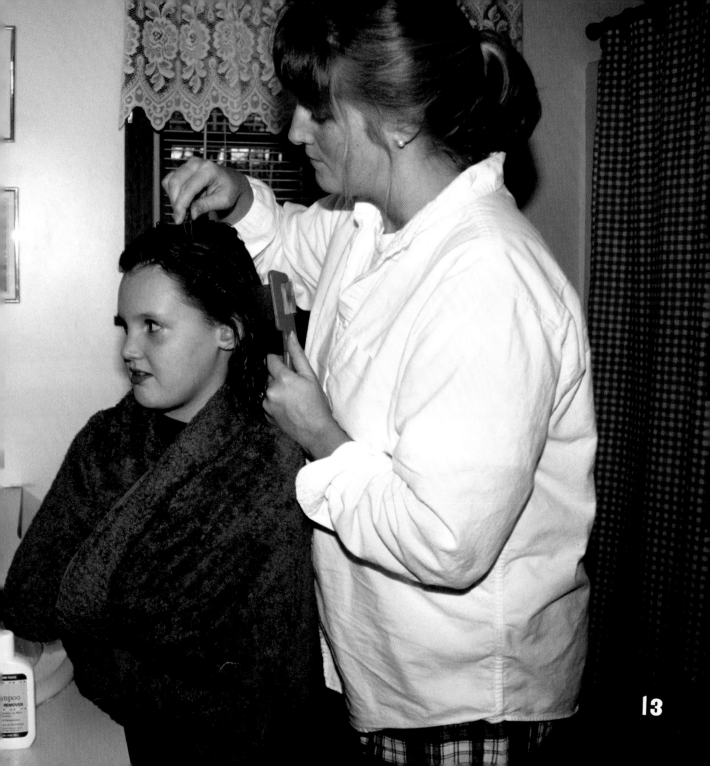

How to Treat Head Lice

You can buy products to help get rid of head lice. Head lice combs remove nits and lice. Head lice **shampoos** have chemicals to kill head lice.

You can take other steps to kill head lice. Vacuuming is the best way to get rid of lice on carpet and rugs. Washing clothes with hot water also kills lice.

If It Gets Worse

Head lice can get worse if nits hatch. Having more lice makes it harder to get rid of them.

Head lice can also get worse if people scratch their heads too hard. Germs can get into the skin and make sores.

Fact!
Children get head lice more often than adults do because children often play close to each other.

Staying Healthy

Some steps can be taken to keep head lice from spreading. People should wash their hair and bedsheets often. People should not share hats, combs, or brushes. Parents should check their kids' heads for lice regularly.

! Fact!
Head lice are not new. Dried-up lice and nits have been found on Egyptian mummies.

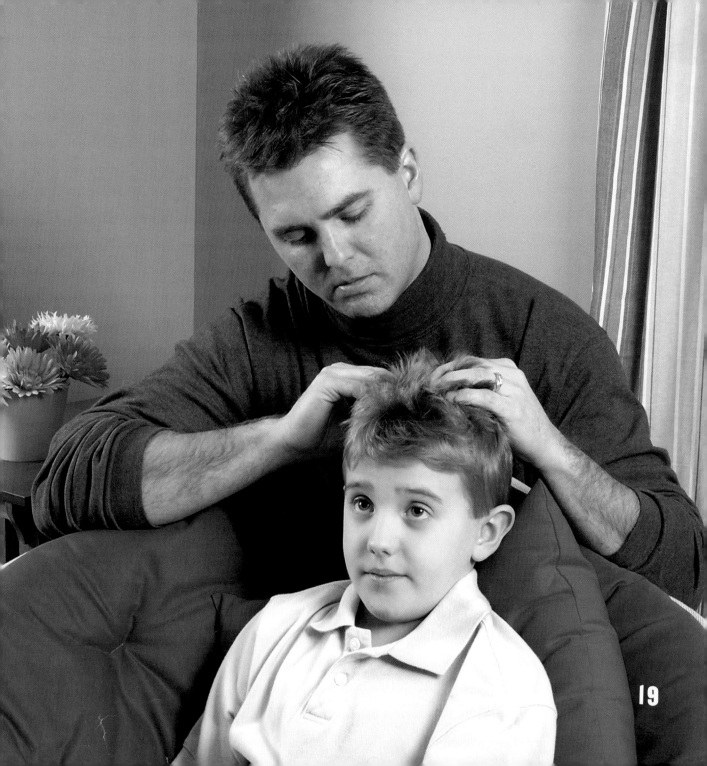

Amazing but True!

Some people don't just eat mayonnaise, they use it to get rid of head lice. Mayonnaise might kill head lice by making it hard for them to breathe. It is unclear how well mayonnaise gets rid of head lice. Mayonnaise is also smelly and hard to wash out of hair. Doctors usually suggest other ways to get rid of head lice that work better and aren't as messy.

Hands On: Hand Comb

Combs with smaller spaces between the teeth can remove lice and nits. Pretend your hand is a comb. See how many "nits" you can pick up.

What You Need
small stones
bucket

What You Do
1. Put the stones in the bucket. Reach into the bucket. Keep your fingers spread apart and hand flat.
2. Lift out as many stones as you can.
3. Count the stones you pulled out.
4. Put the stones back in the bucket. Reach into the bucket again. This time, keep your fingers closer together. Keep your hand flat.
5. Lift out as many stones as you can.
6. Count the stones you pulled out.

Could you lift more stones with your fingers spread apart or together?

Glossary

allergies (AL-uhr-gees)—reactions to things like dogs, cats, and dust; allergies can cause runny noses, sneezing, watery eyes, and itching.

dandruff (DAN-druhf)—tiny white flakes of dead skin

head lice (HED LYSE)—tiny bugs that live in hair; one of these bugs is called a head louse.

nits (NITZ)—lice eggs

shampoo (sham-POO)—a soap or lotion used to wash hair; use head lice shampoos carefully; too much head lice shampoo can make people sick.

Read More

Birch, Robin. *Head Lice Up Close.* Minibeasts Up Close. Chicago: Raintree, 2005.

Lassieur, Allison. *Head Lice.* My Health. New York: Franklin Watts, 2000.

Royston, Angela. *Head Lice.* It's Catching. Chicago: Heinemann, 2002.

Internet Sites

FactHound offers a safe, fun way to find Internet sites related to this book. All of the sites on FactHound have been researched by our staff.

Here's how:
1. Visit *www.facthound.com*
2. Type in this special code **0736842918** for age-appropriate sites. Or enter a search word related to this book for a more general search.
3. Click on the **Fetch It** button.

FactHound will fetch the best sites for you!

Index